The Digital Renaissance

The Digital Renaissance

How Technology is Reviving Artistic Expression

B. Vincent

QuantumQuill Press

CONTENTS

1 Chapter 1: Introduction to the Digital Renaissance 1

2 Chapter 2: The Fusion of Art and Technology 5

3 Chapter 3: Democratizing Creativity 10

4 Chapter 4: Challenges and Opportunities 15

5 Chapter 5: Conclusion 20

Chapter 1: Introduction to the Digital Renaissance

Characterizing the Computerized Renaissance

In the steadily developing scene of craftsmanship and innovation, the idea of the Computerized Renaissance arises as a reference point of development and rehash. This starting section sets the stage by diving into the pith of the Computerized Renaissance and explaining its significant importance inside the contemporary workmanship world. Similarly as the Renaissance of the fourteenth to seventeenth hundreds of years denoted an essential time of social resurrection and investigation, the Computerized Renaissance embodies a cutting edge resurgence portrayed by the combination of creative articulation and mechanical headway.

Inside this part, we leave on an excursion to disentangle the diverse layers of the Computerized Renaissance, analyzing its center parts and portraying its extraordinary power. Through enlightening talk and smart investigation, we try to get a handle on the embodiment of this peculiarity and its suggestions for craftsmen, lovers, and society at large.

From the democratization of inventive instruments to the democratization of access, the Computerized Renaissance epitomizes a change in perspective that rises above traditional limits, encouraging a unique biological system of development and coordinated effort. As we explore through this part, we welcome perusers to consider the significant ramifications of the Computerized Renaissance and set out on a mission to investigate its immense span of potential outcomes.

Verifiable Setting

To really see the value in the meaning of the Computerized Renaissance, setting out on an excursion through the chronicles of craftsmanship history, following the development of imaginative articulation close by the walk of mechanical progress is fundamental. This part fills in as an enthralling time machine, moving perusers across ages and civilizations to observe the unpredictable exchange among workmanship and innovation.

From the earliest cavern artworks to the works of art of the Renaissance time frame, we reveal the getting through human drive to make and advance, filled by an unquenchable interest and limitless creative mind. From the perspective of history, we gain a more profound comprehension of how mechanical headways — whether the innovation of the print machine or the appearance of photography — have consistently reshaped the creative scene, testing shows and rousing new types of articulation.

As we navigate the hundreds of years, we witness urgent snapshots of intermingling among craftsmanship and innovation, each making a permanent imprint on the direction of human innovativeness. From the Modern Upset to the Data Age, the narrative of workmanship is unyieldingly entwined with the tale of mechanical development, finishing in the Computerized Renaissance — a turning point that proclaims another period of imaginative chance and trial and error.

Through enrapturing accounts and enlightening stories, this part enlightens the rich embroidery of history that has laid the basis for the Computerized Renaissance, welcoming perusers to ponder the significant tradition of the past and its persevering through effect on the current second. As we set out on this verifiable odyssey, we gain a freshly discovered appreciation for the extraordinary force of innovation in molding the course of creative development.

The Effect of Innovation

In this crucial section, we dive profound into the groundbreaking force of innovation and its significant effect on imaginative practice. From the approach of computerized apparatuses to the expansion of vivid encounters, we investigate how headways in innovation have changed the manner in which craftsmen make, team up, and associate with crowds all over the planet.

The computerized domain has turned into a jungle gym of boundless chance, offering craftsmen an extensive material whereupon to release their inventiveness. Through computerized painting, 3D displaying, and augmented reality, craftsmen are not generally limited by the limitations of conventional mediums, yet rather enabled to push the limits of their creative mind to remarkable levels. We look at how these computerized devices have democratized the inventive approach, making craftsmanship more available and comprehensive than any time in recent memory.

In any case, the effect of innovation reaches out a long ways past the domain of creation — it has likewise changed how workmanship is capable and consumed. Intelligent workmanship establishments obscure the line between the physical and computerized universes, welcoming watchers to draw in with the craftsmanship and become piece of the story effectively. We dig into the vivid force of these establishments and their capacity to summon close to home reactions and incite thought.

Besides, innovation has led to new methods of joint effort and local area building, rising above geological limits and encouraging a worldwide trade of thoughts. Online stages and networks furnish craftsmen with a virtual stage to exhibit their work, team up with peers, and draw in with crowds continuously.

As we explore through the heap manners by which innovation has reshaped imaginative articulation, we come to see the value in the Computerized Renaissance as not one minute in time, but rather a change in perspective that keeps on unfurling before our eyes. Through spellbinding stories and quick examination, we enlighten the groundbreaking force of innovation in reviving the imaginative scene and introducing another period of inventive chance.

Outline of the Book

As we close this starting section, we offer an all encompassing perspective on the excursion ahead — an excursion through the core of the Computerized Renaissance and its horde signs in the contemporary workmanship world. Through the sections that follow, we will dive further into the complexities of this peculiarity, investigating its subtleties, difficulties, and open doors.

Section by part, we will set out on a journey of disclosure, from the combination of workmanship and innovation to the democratization of inventiveness, and from the difficulties and chances of the computerized age to the future bearings of the Computerized Renaissance. En route, we will experience charming contextual investigations, intriguing examination, and enlightening bits of knowledge from specialists, researchers, and trend-setters at the front of this groundbreaking development.

From the perspective of history, hypothesis, and practice, we will look to unwind the secrets of the Computerized Renaissance and gain a more profound comprehension of its significant ramifications for the eventual fate of craftsmanship and society. From the democratization of imaginative instruments to the moral contemplations of advanced safe-guarding, we will explore the perplexing territory of the computerized scene with interest and understanding.

As we set out on this scholarly odyssey, we welcome perusers to go along with us in investigating the boondocks of creative articulation and mechanical development, and to take part in an exchange that rises above limits of time, space, and medium. Together, let us leave on an excursion of disclosure — an excursion to the core of the Computerized Renaissance.

Chapter 2: The Fusion of Art and Technology

Advanced Instruments and Methods

Inside the huge territory of the advanced domain, craftsmen use an arms stockpile of state of the art apparatuses and methods to reinvigorate their inventive dreams. In this part, we set out on an excursion through the computerized scene, investigating the heap manners by which innovation has reformed the imaginative cycle.

Computerized painting arises as a foundation of present day imaginative articulation, offering craftsmen a range of limitless conceivable outcomes and a material unbounded by the requirements of the actual world. Through the consistent combination of customary creative standards and advanced development, specialists bridle the force of computerized brushes, layers, and impacts to make vivid universes that dazzle the creative mind.

Past the domain of two-layered workmanship, we dive into the domain of 3D demonstrating and movement, where craftsmen shape computerized dirt with accuracy and artfulness to rejuvenate their manifestations in three-layered space. From character plan to building perception, the domain of 3D craftsmanship opens up a domain of boundless potential, obscuring the limits among the real world and dream.

What's more, as we adventure further into the computerized outskirts, we experience the vivid universe of computer generated reality — a domain where craftsmanship rises above the bounds of the screen and wraps the watcher in an intuitive tactile encounter. Using VR headsets and movement regulators, specialists make vivid universes that welcome watchers to step inside and become dynamic members in the creative story.

As we explore through the rich embroidered artwork of advanced apparatuses and methods, we take the stand concerning the groundbreaking influence of innovation in reshaping the imaginative scene and extending the skylines of inventive chance. Through charming models and clever investigation, we gain a more profound appreciation for the cooperative connection among workmanship and innovation, and the vast possible that lies at the convergence of the two.

Cooperative Stages

In the interconnected advanced age, joint effort exceeds all logical limitations. This part investigates the powerful biological system of online stages and networks that act as prolific ground for cooperative creative undertakings. From the perspective of virtual coordinated effort, we witness the separating of topographical hindrances and the development of worldwide imaginative networks joined by a common enthusiasm for inventiveness.

Online stages, for example, web-based entertainment organizations, craftsmanship discussions, and cooperative stages give specialists a virtual stage to grandstand their work, draw in with friends, and look for motivation from a different cluster of voices and viewpoints. Whether through virtual displays or online presentations, specialists can associate with crowds all over the planet, rising above the impediments of actual reality.

Besides, cooperative stages encourage a feeling of co-creation and aggregate development, where specialists meet up to team up on projects that push the limits of imaginative articulation. From advanced workmanship groups to cooperative craftsmanship games, these stages act as hatcheries for trial and error and investigation, permitting specialists to pool their gifts and assets to make an option that could be more prominent than the amount of its parts.

Through enthralling contextual analyses and firsthand records, we dive into the groundbreaking force of cooperative stages in molding the contemporary workmanship scene. From grassroots developments to worldwide coordinated efforts, we give testimony regarding the significant effect of innovation in encouraging association, local area, and imaginative cooperation on an uncommon scale. As we explore through this section, we gain a more profound appreciation for the force of coordinated effort to rise above limits and manufacture significant associations in the computerized age.

Intuitive Workmanship Establishments

In this enamoring investigation, we adventure into the domain of intuitive workmanship establishments, where innovation fills in as a conductor for vivid tactile encounters that obscure the limits between the physical and computerized universes. From intuitive models to expanded reality establishments, we take the stand concerning the extraordinary force of innovation in reshaping the manner in which we draw in with craftsmanship.

Intelligent craftsmanship establishments welcome watchers to become dynamic members in the imaginative cycle, welcoming them to contact, control, and even shape the fine art itself. Using sensors, cameras, and movement following innovation, specialists establish dynamic conditions that answer the developments and tokens of the watcher, changing the demonstration of perception into an intuitive exchange between the craftsmanship and the crowd.

Through charming stories and firsthand records, we investigate the assorted scope of intuitive workmanship establishments that have spellbound crowds all over the planet. From vivid soundscapes to intelligent projections, these establishments push the limits of creative articulation, welcoming watchers to draw in with workmanship in new and unforeseen ways.

Besides, intuitive workmanship establishments act as an impetus for investigation and disclosure, welcoming watchers to investigate subjects of personality, insight, and the human experience. Through intuitive narrating and vivid conditions, specialists make instinctive encounters that reverberate on a profoundly close to home level, cultivating associations and encouraging compassion in manners that conventional works of art can't.

As we explore through the hypnotizing universe of intuitive craftsmanship establishments, we gain a more profound appreciation for the extraordinary force of innovation in reshaping the imaginative scene and pushing the limits of innovative articulation. Through charming models and astute examination, we come to grasp the significant effect of intuitive workmanship in testing our discernments, igniting interest, and rousing miracle in the advanced age.

Contextual investigations

Inside the domain of the combination of craftsmanship and innovation, contextual analyses act as enlightening windows into the inventive personalities and inventive strategies of specialists who have effectively coordinated innovation into their creative practice. In this part, we leave on an excursion through a progression of dazzling contextual investigations, each offering exceptional experiences into the manners by which innovation has changed creative articulation.

From pioneers in computerized craftsmanship to contemporary visionaries pushing the limits of augmented reality, we investigate crafted by specialists who have embraced innovation as a device for imagination and development. Through inside and out examinations and firsthand records, we gain a more profound comprehension of the inspirations, motivations, and difficulties looked by these exploring specialists as they explore the computerized boondocks.

Through enrapturing models going from advanced painting to intelligent establishments, we witness the horde manners by which innovation has altered the creative interaction, opening up new roads for trial and error and investigation. Whether using computer based intelligence calculations or state of the art programming devices, these specialists saddle the force of innovation to understand their imaginative dreams in manners that were once unbelievable.

Also, these contextual investigations act as wellsprings of motivation and direction for hopeful craftsmen trying to explore the crossing point of workmanship and innovation. Through the tales of these spearheading specialists, we gain important bits of knowledge into the potential outcomes and entanglements of coordinating innovation into imaginative work on, offering a guide for those setting out on their own inventive excursions in the computerized age.

As we venture through these dazzling contextual investigations, we come to see the value in the significant effect of innovation on the contemporary workmanship scene, and the unfathomable possible that lies at the convergence of craftsmanship and innovation. From the perspective of these visionary specialists, we gain a more profound comprehension of the groundbreaking force of innovation in reshaping the manner in which we make, insight, and draw in with workmanship in the computerized age.

3 |

Chapter 3: Democratizing Creativity

Openness of Apparatuses

In the dynamic scene of imaginative creation, admittance to devices and assets has for quite some time been a characterizing factor in the capacity to rejuvenate innovative dreams. In any case, in the computerized age, innovation has arisen as a strong balancer, democratizing admittance to imaginative devices and making everything fair for hopeful makers around the world.

This part dives into the extraordinary effect of innovation in separating boundaries to passage and making imaginative devices more open to a more extensive crowd than any other time in recent memory. Through the multiplication of advanced programming applications, hopeful craftsmen can now saddle similar amazing assets utilized by experts, from computerized painting programming to 3D displaying programs.

Besides, headways in equipment innovation, like realistic tablets and touchscreen gadgets, have additionally democratized the inventive strategy, giving specialists natural and reasonable apparatuses for rejuvenating their thoughts. At this point not obliged by the restrictive expenses of conventional workmanship supplies, hopeful makers can investigate their innovativeness unafraid of monetary obstructions.

Through dazzling models and firsthand records, we witness the significant effect of innovation in democratizing admittance to imaginative devices and enabling makers from assorted foundations to understand their innovative dreams. From advanced painting to liveliness, craftsmen all over the planet are outfitting the influence of innovation to put themselves out there in new and creative ways, enhancing the worldwide social scene simultaneously.

As we explore through this section, we gain a more profound appreciation for the groundbreaking force of innovation in democratizing imagination and enabling people to open their creative potential. From the perspective of openness, we come to comprehend the significant ramifications of innovation in reshaping the manner in which we make, insight, and draw in with craftsmanship in the advanced age.

Internet Learning and Instructional exercises

In the powerful scene of imaginative training, the computerized age has introduced another time of democratization, enabling hopeful makers to get to an abundance of information and skill from the solace of their own homes. This part dives into the extraordinary job of web based learning stages and instructional exercises in democratizing imaginative schooling and expertise advancement.

Through the expansion of internet learning stages like YouTube, Skillshare, and Udemy, hopeful specialists have remarkable admittance to a huge swath of instructional exercises, courses, and assets covering many imaginative disciplines. From computerized painting strategies to 3D displaying instructional exercises, these stages offer an abundance of chances for craftsmen to grow their ranges of abilities and investigate new mediums.

Besides, the intuitive idea of internet learning permits hopeful craftsmen to learn at their own speed, stopping, rewinding, and returning to examples depending on the situation to build up their comprehension and dominance of creative procedures. Whether a beginner trying to get familiar with the essentials or an old pro hoping to refine their abilities, internet learning stages give an adaptable and open road for creative development and improvement.

Through enrapturing contextual analyses and firsthand records, we witness the extraordinary effect of web based advancing in engaging specialists from different foundations to open their imaginative potential and seek after their interests. From self-trained specialists desiring experts, specialists all over the planet are outfitting the force of internet figuring out how to sharpen their art and understand their creative yearnings.

As we explore through this section, we gain a more profound appreciation for the democratizing force of innovation in giving fair admittance to creative schooling and expertise improvement. From the perspective of web based learning, we come to comprehend the significant effect of innovation in evening the odds and enabling hopeful makers to seek after their fantasies in the advanced age.

Crowdfunding and Support

In the conventional craftsmanship world, getting subsidizing for imaginative undertakings frequently introduced an imposing boundary for arising specialists, expecting admittance to monetary assets and laid out organizations of help. Nonetheless, in the advanced age, innovation has upset the scene of imaginative subsidizing, democratizing admittance to monetary help through the ascent of crowdfunding stages and online support.

This part investigates the extraordinary effect of crowdfunding stages like Kickstarter, Indiegogo, and Patreon in engaging specialists to subsidize their undertakings and associate with benefactors straightforwardly. Through these stages, specialists can feature their work, articulate their imaginative vision, and request support from a worldwide crowd of benefactors and allies.

Besides, crowdfunding stages offer specialists a stage to connect straightforwardly with their crowd, cultivating a feeling of local area and association that rises above customary limits of geology and societal position. By offering prizes and motivations to benefactors, specialists can develop a feeling of pride and interest in their imaginative under-takings, fashioning significant associations with allies that stretch out past simple monetary exchanges.

Through dazzling contextual analyses and firsthand records, we witness the groundbreaking force of crowdfunding in empowering craftsmen to rejuvenate their imaginative dreams and seek after projects that could somehow have stayed hidden. From free producers to sight and sound craftsmen, makers from different disciplines are saddling the force of crowdfunding to fund their tasks and construct a faithful fan base all the while.

As we explore through this part, we gain a more profound appreciation for the democratizing effect of innovation in giving evenhanded admittance to monetary help for specialists of all foundations and disciplines. From the perspective of crowdfunding and support, we come to comprehend the significant ramifications of innovation in reshaping the financial aspects of workmanship and enabling makers to seek after their interests in the computerized age.

Variety and Inclusivity

In the computerized time, innovation has arisen as a strong power for enhancing different voices and points of view inside the craftsmanship world, encouraging a culture of inclusivity and portrayal. This part dives into the extraordinary capability of innovation in growing the extent of imaginative articulation and testing conventional thoughts of personality and portrayal.

Through the democratizing force of computerized stages and web-based entertainment organizations, craftsmen from underrepresented networks have tracked down a stage to share their accounts, praise their societies, and challenge winning stories of minimization and rejection. From LGBTQ+ specialists to craftsmen of variety, the computerized domain offers a space for minimized voices to be heard and celebrated, encouraging a more comprehensive and various creative scene.

Additionally, progressions in innovation have empowered specialists to investigate subjects of character and portrayal in new and imaginative ways, utilizing advanced devices and stages to make craftsmanship that mirrors the rich embroidered artwork of human experience. From computerized narrating to intelligent establishments, craftsmen are saddling the force of innovation to intensify different voices and viewpoints, moving watchers to defy their own inclinations and suspicions.

Through charming models and firsthand records, we witness the groundbreaking effect of innovation in reshaping the social account and engaging underestimated networks to recover their voices and stories. From online craftsmanship developments to computerized activism, specialists from different foundations are utilizing innovation to impact social change and encourage a more fair and comprehensive society.

As we explore through this section, we gain a more profound appreciation for the democratizing capability of innovation in enhancing different voices and points of view inside the craftsmanship world. From the perspective of variety and inclusivity, we come to figure out the significant effect of innovation in testing fundamental obstructions and cultivating a more comprehensive and delegate creative scene in the computerized age.

4 |

Chapter 4: Challenges and Opportunities

Copyright and Possession

In the unique scene of the computerized age, the topic of copyright and proprietorship arises as a complicated and multi-layered challenge for craftsmen and makers. This section dives into the complexities of intellectual property regulation and licensed innovation freedoms with regards to computerized workmanship, investigating the difficulties and valuable open doors introduced by the advanced medium.

As innovation empowers the simple multiplication and circulation of computerized fine arts, craftsmen face a horde of difficulties in safeguarding their imaginative privileges and stating responsibility for work. From issues of counterfeiting and unapproved propagation to the double-dealing of computerized content without legitimate attribution, specialists should explore a complex lawful scene to shield their protected innovation.

Besides, the decentralized idea of the web presents special difficulties in implementing intellectual property regulation and shielding advanced content from encroachment. With the expansion of online stages and web-based entertainment organizations, specialists should stay watchful in checking their advanced impression and going to proactive lengths to safeguard their work from unapproved use.

Through enthralling contextual investigations and firsthand records, we witness this present reality ramifications of copyright encroachment and protected innovation robbery on specialists and makers. From autonomous craftsmen to laid out experts, makers of all foundations wrestle with the test of declaring their freedoms and safeguarding their work in the advanced age.

Nonetheless, in the midst of these difficulties lie amazing open doors for development and imagination. As craftsmen investigate better approaches for appropriating and adapting their work in the advanced domain, new models of possession and cooperation arise, testing customary ideas of copyright and licensed innovation. From the perspective of copyright and proprietorship, we come to comprehend the significant ramifications of innovation in reshaping the elements of imaginative possession and creative articulation in the advanced age.

Computerized Safeguarding

In the steadily developing scene of computerized craftsmanship, the safeguarding of fine arts arises as quite difficult for specialists and social organizations the same. This section dives into the significance of computerized safeguarding and the intricacies engaged with guaranteeing the life span and availability of advanced craftsmanships for people in the future.

Not at all like customary works of art, which are many times saved through actual means, for example, exhibition halls and displays, computerized craftsmanships exist in a continually moving and fleeting computerized climate. As innovation develops and document designs become outdated, advanced works of art are in danger of being lost or debased over the long haul, presenting critical difficulties for craftsmen trying to safeguard their imaginative heritage.

Through enthralling contextual analyses and firsthand records, we investigate the horde manners by which craftsmen and social foundations are wrestling with the test of advanced protection. From the advancement of open principles and best practices to the foundation of computerized files and protection drives, partners across the craftsmanship world are working resolutely to shield computerized fine arts for people in the future.

Additionally, the ascent of blockchain innovation offers new open doors for guaranteeing the uprightness and credibility of computerized works of art through decentralized and sealed records. By recording the provenance and possession history of computerized craftsmanships on the blockchain, specialists can lay out a safe and unchanging record of their inventive result, guaranteeing that their work stays in salvageable shape and open into the indefinite future.

As we explore through this part, we gain a more profound appreciation for the intricacies engaged with computerized protection and the significance of addressing these difficulties to guarantee the drawn out reasonability of computerized craftsmanship. From the perspective of advanced protection, we come to comprehend the significant ramifications of innovation in reshaping our way to deal with saving and defending creative legacy in the computerized age.

Moral Contemplations

In the computerized scene, the convergence of innovation and craftsmanship delivers a bunch of moral contemplations that request cautious assessment and reflection. This part dives into the moral ramifications of innovation in craftsmanship, examining issues, for example, observation, protection concerns, and the commodification of imagination.

As innovation turns out to be progressively incorporated into imaginative practice, inquiries of protection and reconnaissance pose a potential threat. With the expansion of advanced stages and web-based entertainment organizations, craftsmen should wrestle with the ramifications of sharing individual data and innovative substance on the web. From worries about information protection to the potential for algorithmic predisposition and observation, craftsmen should explore a complex moral territory in the computerized age.

Besides, the commodification of inventiveness brings up moral issues about the commercialization of workmanship and the double-dealing of specialists' work. As computerized stages and commercial centers work with the trading of advanced craftsmanships, specialists should fight with issues of fair remuneration, copyright encroachment, and the debasement of imaginative work. The ascent of NFTs (non-fungible tokens) further muddles these moral contemplations, bringing up issues about proprietorship, validness, and natural effect.

Through enthralling contextual investigations and firsthand records, we witness this present reality ramifications of these moral difficulties on specialists and makers. From worries about information protection and algorithmic predisposition to banters about the morals of NFTs and blockchain innovation, craftsmen from assorted foundations wrestle with the ethical intricacies of innovation in workmanship.

As we explore through this section, we gain a more profound appreciation for the moral contemplations intrinsic in the crossing point of innovation and workmanship. From the perspective of morals, we come to figure out the significant ramifications of innovation in molding our qualities, standards, and ways of behaving in the advanced age, and the basic of moving toward mechanical development with care and basic reflection.

Future Headings

As we stand at the cliff of the advanced age, the fate of craftsmanship and innovation holds unfathomable conceivable outcomes and undiscovered possibility. This section conjectures on the future bearings of the Advanced Renaissance and the potential directions that innovation and workmanship might require in the years to come.

From the joining of computerized reasoning and AI into imaginative practice to the investigation of virtual and expanded reality as vivid mechanisms for inventive articulation, the fate of craftsmanship vows to be both invigorating and groundbreaking. As innovation proceeds to develop and grow, specialists will have exceptional chances to push the limits of imaginative advancement and investigate new wildernesses of innovativeness.

In addition, the democratizing force of innovation offers new roads for encouraging inclusivity and variety inside the craftsmanship world, enhancing minimized voices and testing winning accounts of prohibition. As advanced stages and online entertainment networks democratize admittance to creative assets and open doors, specialists from different foundations will have more prominent perceivability and portrayal, enhancing the worldwide social scene simultaneously.

In any case, in the midst of the commitment of progress and development, difficulties and vulnerabilities remain. From worries about information protection and reconnaissance to banters about the moral ramifications of arising innovations, specialists and makers should explore a complex and consistently changing scene laden with moral and moral problems.

Through speculative examination and informed projection, we gain experiences into the potential bearings that innovation and craftsmanship might take from here on out. From the ascent of vivid encounters and intelligent establishments to the democratization of imaginative instruments and assets, the fate of the Computerized Renaissance vows to be a dynamic and groundbreaking excursion into unfamiliar domain.

As we explore through this part, we gain a more profound appreciation for the groundbreaking force of innovation in reshaping the scene of imaginative articulation and the limitless expected that lies at the crossing point of workmanship and innovation. From the perspective of future headings, we come to figure out the basic of embracing mechanical development with transparency, interest, and a feeling of investigation as we diagram the course for the fate of workmanship in the computerized age.

5

Chapter 5: Conclusion

Rundown of Central issues

As we finish up our investigation of the Computerized Renaissance, it is fundamental to think about the vital subjects and contentions that have arisen all through our excursion. This section fills in as a snapshot of blend, uniting the different strings of our conversation to distil the fundamental experiences and focus points from our investigation of the convergence of workmanship and innovation.

All through the former sections, we have dug into the groundbreaking force of innovation in reshaping imaginative articulation and testing customary ideas of innovativeness. From the combination of craftsmanship and innovation to the democratization of imagination, we have seen how progressions in computerized apparatuses and stages have democratized admittance to creative assets, cultivated new methods of coordinated effort, and enhanced assorted voices and points of view inside the workmanship world.

Also, we have wrestled with the moral ramifications of innovation in workmanship, from worries about information security and reconnaissance to banters about the commodification of imagination and the morals of arising advances, for example, blockchain and NFTs. Through smart examination and thoughtfulness, we have stood up to the ethical intricacies of innovation in craftsmanship and the basic of moving toward mechanical advancement with care and basic reflection.

As we consider the Computerized Renaissance, we are helped to remember the extraordinary capability of innovation to democratize imagination, encourage inclusivity and variety, and push the limits of creative advancement. In any case, we are likewise helped to remember the moral difficulties and vulnerabilities that go with mechanical advancement, and the obligation we bear as makers and buyers to explore these intricacies with trustworthiness and empathy.

In this rundown of central issues, we welcome perusers to ponder the bits of knowledge and examples gained from our investigation of the Advanced Renaissance and to think about the ramifications of innovation for the fate of craftsmanship and society. As we set out on this excursion of reflection, we are helped to remember the significant effect of the Computerized Renaissance on imaginative articulation and the persevering through inheritance it leaves on the social scene of the 21st 100 years.

Reflection on the Computerized Renaissance

As we consider the Computerized Renaissance and its significant effect on creative articulation, we are constrained to stop and think about the more extensive ramifications of this extraordinary development. All through our investigation, we have seen the rise of another time portrayed by the combination of craftsmanship and innovation — a renaissance of imagination that rises above customary limits and difficulties traditional thoughts of creative practice.

The Computerized Renaissance addresses not simply a mechanical upset, but rather a social resurrection — a seismic change in the manner we make, consume, and draw in with craftsmanship in the advanced age. From the democratization of innovative apparatuses to the expansion of online stages and networks, we have seen how innovation has democratized admittance to imaginative assets and enabled makers from assorted foundations to impart their accounts and points of view to the world.

Besides, the Computerized Renaissance has cultivated new methods of cooperation and local area building, rising above geological limits and encouraging a worldwide trade of thoughts and motivation. Through the interconnected snare of computerized stages and interpersonal organizations, specialists have tracked down new roads for associating with crowds, working together with peers, and enhancing their voices in the social discussion.

However, in the midst of the commitment of progress and development, we are additionally faced with moral predicaments and difficulties that request our consideration and reflection. From worries about information security and observation to banters about the commercialization of imagination, the Computerized Renaissance compels us to stand up to the ethical intricacies of innovation in workmanship and the obligation we bear as makers and shoppers to explore these intricacies with honesty and empathy.

As we ponder the Advanced Renaissance, we are helped to remember the groundbreaking force of innovation to reshape the imaginative scene and push the limits of inventive articulation. In any case, we are likewise helped to remember the basic of moving toward mechanical development with care and basic reflection, and the obligation we bear to guarantee that innovation fills in as a power for good in the realm of workmanship and then some.

In this reflection on the Advanced Renaissance, we are welcome to ponder the significant effect of innovation on imaginative articulation and the getting through heritage it leaves on the social scene of the 21st hundred years. Through thoughtfulness and request, we come to comprehend the meaning of this groundbreaking development and the potential it holds to shape the eventual fate of workmanship and society for a long time into the future.

Source of inspiration

As we finish up our investigation of the Computerized Renaissance, we are called upon to embrace innovation as a device for innovativeness and development, and to keep investigating the crossing point of workmanship and innovation with interest and liberality. This section fills in as a source of inspiration, encouraging perusers to tackle the force of innovation to release their imaginative potential and shape the fate of workmanship in the computerized age.

In a period set apart by fast mechanical headway and uncommon network, we have the chance to rethink the limits of creative articulation and rock the boat. By embracing computerized instruments and stages, we can democratize admittance to imaginative assets, intensify different voices and viewpoints, and cultivate a more comprehensive and lively creative local area.

Additionally, we are called upon to take part in basic discourse and reflection on the moral ramifications of innovation in craftsmanship, and to advocate for mindful and moral utilization of innovation in the inventive approach. From advancing information protection and computerized security to supporting variety and portrayal in the workmanship world, we have an obligation to guarantee that innovation fills in as a power for good and strengthening in the realm of craftsmanship and then some.

As makers and shoppers of craftsmanship, we are called upon to be aware of the effect of our activities and decisions on the more extensive social scene. By supporting craftsmen and social establishments that embrace innovation as an instrument for innovativeness and development, we can add to the proceeded with development and advancement of the Computerized Renaissance and shape a future where craftsmanship is more open, comprehensive, and effective than any time in recent memory.

In this source of inspiration, we are helped to remember the groundbreaking capability of innovation to alter the manner in which we make, insight, and draw in with craftsmanship in the computerized age. Through aggregate activity and cooperation, we have the ability to shape the fate of workmanship and society for a long time into the future. As we leave on this excursion of investigation and disclosure, we are roused to embrace the Computerized Renaissance as an impetus for positive change and an encouraging sign for the eventual fate of workmanship and humankind.

Last Contemplations

As we draw our excursion through the Computerized Renaissance to a nearby, we are left with a significant feeling of stunningness and marvel at the extraordinary force of innovation to reshape the imaginative scene and reclassify the limits of innovativeness. This last part offers a snapshot of reflection — an opportunity to stop and consider the meaning of our investigation and the persevering through tradition of the Computerized Renaissance.

In our investigation of the convergence of workmanship and innovation, we have seen the development of another worldview — a renaissance of imagination that rises above conventional limits and engages craftsmen to understand their innovative dreams in manners that were once impossible. From the democratization of imaginative apparatuses to the enhancement of assorted voices and points of view, the Advanced Renaissance has reformed the manner in which we make, insight, and draw in with craftsmanship in the computerized age.

However, as we ponder the excursion we have embraced, we are reminded that the Computerized Renaissance isn't one minute in time, yet a continuous cycle — an excursion of investigation and disclosure that keeps on unfurling before our eyes. As innovation develops and progresses, so too does the scene of imaginative articulation, offering new open doors and difficulties for specialists and makers to explore.

In our last considerations, we are helped to remember the obligation we bear as overseers of this extraordinary development — to steward the Computerized Renaissance with care and expectation, and to guarantee that it fills in as a power for positive change and strengthening in the realm of workmanship and then some. By embracing innovation as a device for imagination and development, and by supporting for moral and mindful utilization of innovation in the innovative strategy, we can shape a future where workmanship is more open, comprehensive, and effective than any time in recent memory.

All things being equal, we are loaded up with a feeling of idealism and energy for the fate of craftsmanship in the computerized age. As we leave on this excursion of investigation and revelation, we are propelled to embrace the Computerized Renaissance as a demonstration of the endless capability of human inventiveness and resourcefulness, and an encouraging sign for the eventual fate of craftsmanship and mankind. Through our aggregate endeavors and obligation to development and greatness, we can guarantee that the tradition of the Computerized Renaissance perseveres for a long time into the future, molding a future where craftsmanship is a wellspring of motivation, reflection, and change for all.